SPEED MACHINES

AUDI

Julia J. Quinlan

PowerKiDS press.

New York

Published in 2014 by The Rosen Publishing Group, Inc.
29 East 21st Street, New York, NY 10010

First Edition

Editor: Jennifer Way
Book Design: Greg Tucker
Book Layout: Kate Vlachos

Photo Credits: Cover © Hans Dieter Seufert/c/age fotostock; pp. 4, 24, 25 (bottom), 29 Darren Brode/Shutterstock.com; p. 5 (top) Indigo/Getty Images Entertainment/Getty Images; p. 5 (bottom) Vibrant Image Studio/Shutterstock.com; pp. 6, 23, 27 KENCKO photography/Shutterstock.com; p. 7 Sean Nel/Shutterstock.com; p. 9 Bocman1973/Shutterstock.com; pp. 10, 21 Dongliu/Shutterstock.com; p. 11 (top) Maxene Huiyu/Shutterstock.com; p. 11 (bottom) TonyV3112/Shutterstock.com; pp. 12, 26 Bloomberg/Getty Images; pp. 13, 17 de2marco/Shutterstock.com; pp. 14, 15 Max Earey/Shutterstock.com; p. 16 Ralph Orlowski/Getty Images News/Getty Images; p. 18 Maksim Toome/Shutterstock.com; p. 19 Philip Lange/Shutterstock.com; p. 20 © Transtock/SuperStock; p. 25 (top) Christoff/Shutterstock.com; p. 28 Kevin Pharry/Stringer/WireImage/Getty Images.

Library of Congress Cataloging-in-Publication Data

Quinlan, Julia J.
 Audi / by Julia J. Quinlan. — First edition.
      pages cm. — (Speed machines)
 Includes index.
 ISBN 978-1-4777-0810-1 (library binding) — ISBN 978-1-4777-0992-4 (paperback) —
 ISBN 978-1-4777-0993-1 (6-pack)
 1. Audi automobile—Juvenile literature. I. Title.
 TL215.A8Q85 2014
 629.222—dc23
                                    2013001127

Manufactured in the United States of America

CPSIA Compliance Information: Batch #S13PK8: For Further Information contact Rosen Publishing, New York, New York at 1-800-237-9932

Contents

Audi Excellence

The logo of the German car company Audi is four overlapping rings. These four rings represent the four companies that came together in the 1930s to form Audi. Each of the four companies was an **innovator**. Combined they made what would become one of the most respected car brands in the world. Today, Audi is known for its eye-catching, powerful sports cars. It is also known for its **engineering**. Audis are built to last.

The A3 is Audi's compact car model.

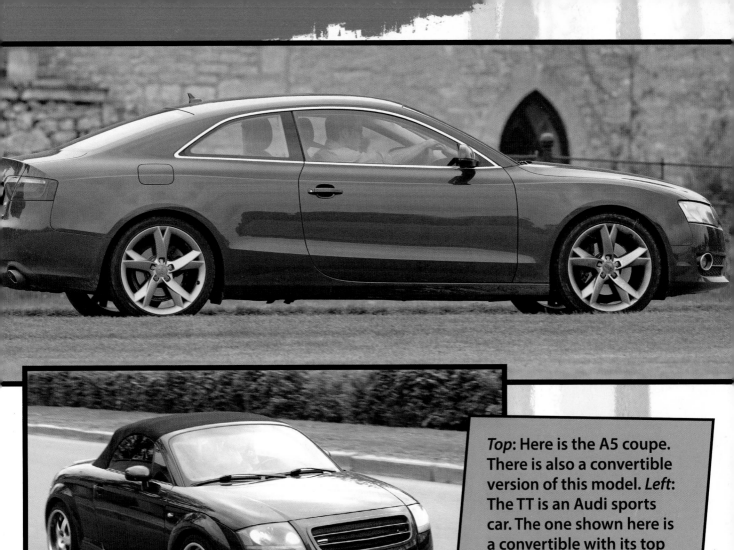

Top: Here is the A5 coupe. There is also a convertible version of this model. *Left*: The TT is an Audi sports car. The one shown here is a convertible with its top pulled up.

Audi has a huge range of cars. **Coupes**, convertibles, **sedans**, SUVs, and **hybrids** are just a few of the vehicles offered by Audi. Each type of vehicle comes with numerous options. There are different engines, different colors, and different prices. Some Audis are really expensive, costing hundreds of thousands of dollars. There are also lower-priced Audis. There is an Audi for everyone!

From Four to One

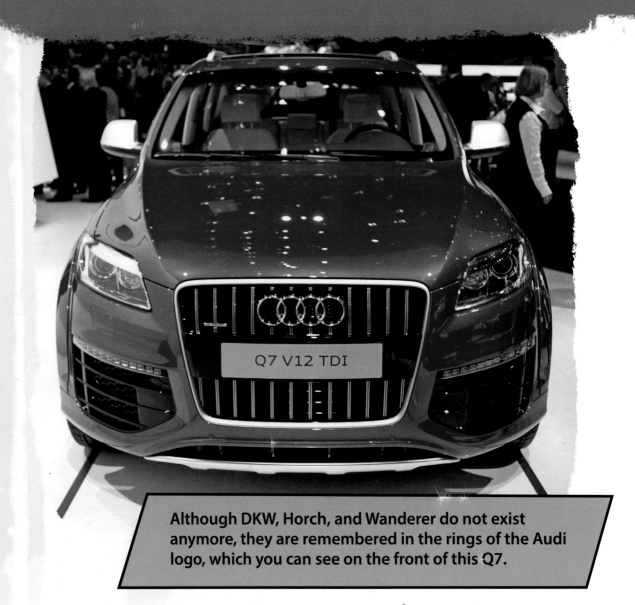

Although DKW, Horch, and Wanderer do not exist anymore, they are remembered in the rings of the Audi logo, which you can see on the front of this Q7.

The four companies that originally made up what is today Audi were, Audi, DKW, Horch, and Wanderer. Each company was an innovator in car manufacturing. The companies were all founded in the late 1800s and early 1900s. At that time, automobiles were a new and exciting **technology**. The companies merged in 1932 under the name Auto Union AG. This merger made the company the second-largest car manufacturer in Germany at the time.

For many years, each of the brands in Auto Union AG kept its name and specialized in a different area. Wanderer made midsize cars. DKW made motorcycles and small cars. Audi made deluxe midsize cars. Horch made top-of-the-line automobiles. In 1965, Auto Union AG retired three of the brand names and began making all of its cars under the Audi brand name. That same year, Audi was bought by Volkswagen. In 1969, another company called NSU joined Audi.

Here is one of the cars made by DKW in the 1930s.

Innovating the Automobile

The founding companies of Audi were making cars when cars were a new idea. They were responsible for many important innovations. In 1926, Horch came out with the first German eight-cylinder engine. The first model to have the eight-cylinder engine was called the Horch 8 Type 303. DKW was the first company to mass-produce a car with front-wheel drive. The DKW F1 Roadster, with front-wheel drive, came out in 1931. Most cars at the time used rear-wheel drive.

Audi and DKW were pioneers in the fields of **aerodynamics** and lightweight construction. Making a car aerodynamic means that when it is moving, air flows over it more easily. That helps the car go faster. Big, boxy cars are not as aerodynamic as small, rounded cars. Audi was experimenting with aerodynamics as early as 1923. The 1923 Type K by Audi had a streamlined aluminum body. Lightweight construction also helps with speed. Lighter cars can **accelerate** faster than heavier cars.

This is a Horch Type 303.

Today's Audis

Audi has always offered its customers many options. Today, Audi has 12 series of cars. They are the A3, the A4, the A5, the A6, the A7, the A8, the allroad, the Q5, the Q7, the TT, the R8, and the S. Within these 12 series, there are several different models, and each of these models varies in style and price.

The most affordable Audi on the market today is the A3. It starts at $27,700. It is a hatchback.

This rear view of an A3 shows the car's hatchback.

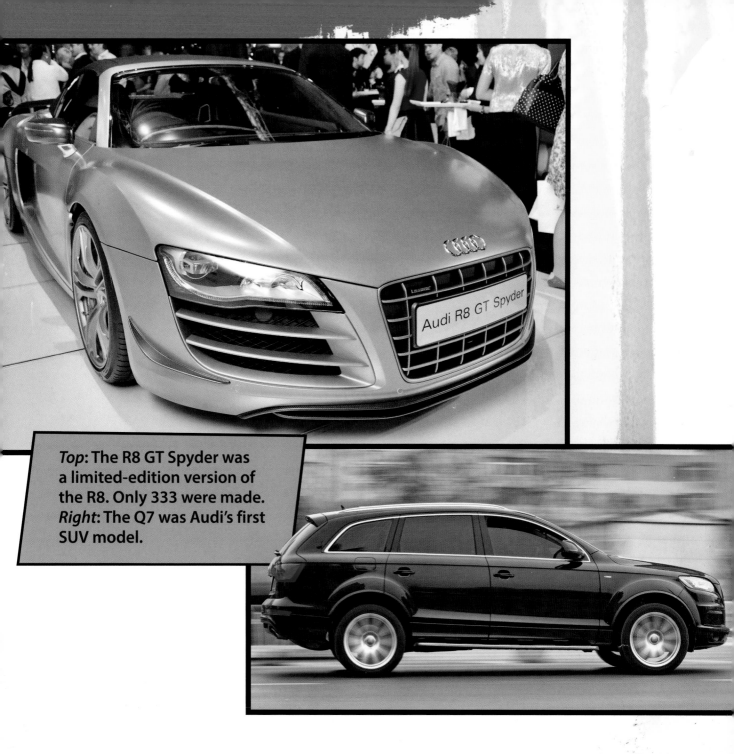

Top: The R8 GT Spyder was a limited-edition version of the R8. Only 333 were made. Right: The Q7 was Audi's first SUV model.

A hatchback has a normal nose but a rectangular back with a large door, or hatch, on the back. Hatchbacks provide lots of room for luggage, groceries, and anything else a driver might need. The A3 has four doors and a top speed of 130 miles per hour (209 km/h). The most expensive Audi available is the R8 GT Spyder. It has a starting price of $210,300 and a top speed of 198 miles per hour (319 km/h).

Rally Racecars

This Audi is being driven on a snowy rally course. Audi's all-wheel drive cars give drivers greater control over the car, especially if there are slippery conditions like there are here.

Audi's most famous racecar was the Audi Quattro. The Audi Quattro was a rally car. Rallies are different from other types of car races because the races are from one point to another and are held on streets, instead of on racetracks. Rally cars look different from **production** cars but are still road legal, unlike racecars. Racecars are so different from sports cars that it is illegal to drive them off the racetrack!

The Audi Quattro was the first rally car to have four-wheel drive. Many companies did not want their cars to have four-wheel drive because they thought it would slow their cars down since it would make them heavier. Audi proved them wrong. The Quattro won many rallies around the world and won the World Rally Championship in 1983.

Here is an Audi Quattro in a 2012 rally.

Racing Endurance

Like many luxury sports car companies, Audi participates in several different kinds of racing competitions. Companies like to take part in races to show how good they are at engineering and how fast they can make their cars. Audi focuses mostly on **endurance** racing. Endurance races are much longer than other races, like NASCAR races. The 24 Hours of Le Mans race goes on for a full day! These long races test how well cars are made because they must go fast for long periods of time. Many cars break down before the race is finished.

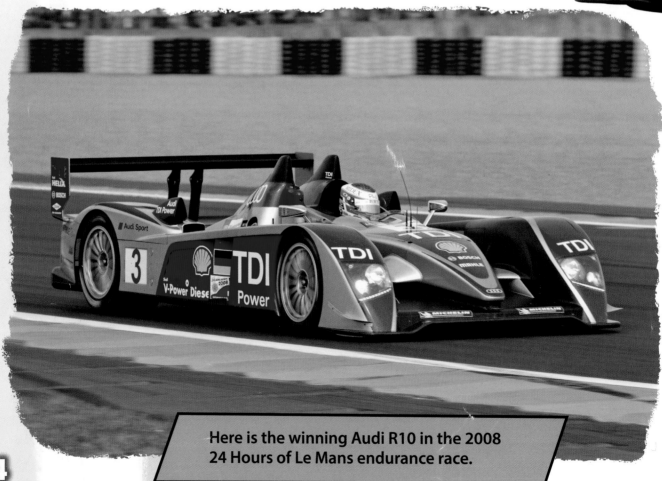

Here is the winning Audi R10 in the 2008 24 Hours of Le Mans endurance race.

The R18 e-tron quattro, shown here, is the hybrid version of the e-tron ultra.

Audi has had much success in endurance racing. Audis won the 24 Hours of Le Mans in 2000, 2001, 2002, 2004, 2005, 2006, 2007, 2008, 2010, 2011, and 2012! In 2012, Audi made history with the Audi R18 e-tron quattro. The Audi R18 e-tron quattro is a hybrid. That means it runs on both gas and electricity. The R18 e-tron quattro became the first hybrid to win at Le Mans.

Audi 80

The Audi 80 was in production from 1966 until 1996. The Audi 80 went by different names. It was called the Audi Fox, the Audi 5+5, the Audi 4000, and the Audi Cabriolet. It was Audi's version of the Volkswagen Passat. It had similar features and components as the Passat. The original Audi 80 was part of a series called F103. Each model in the F103 series was named for its **horsepower**. The Audi 80 had an 80-horsepower engine. The Audi 90 was also in the F103 series. It had a 90-horsepower engine and was a more powerful version of the Audi 80.

The Audi A4, shown here, succeeded the Audi 80. It was first produced in 1994 and continues to be made today.

A4 3.0 TDI quattro

1966 Audi 80

Engine size	1.3 liters
Number of cylinders	4
Transmission	Manual
Gearbox	4 speeds
0–60 mph (0–97 km/h)	14 seconds
Top speed	94 mph (151 km/h)

This vintage, or older model, Audi 80 is being driven in a 2012 demonstration of classic rally cars.

Over the years, the Audi 80 went through many changes. Each new version of the Audi 80 was built on a different platform. The B1 platform ran until 1978, when it was replaced with the B2. In 1986, the B3 platform began, and in 1993 the final platform began, the B4. The different platforms represented changes in the design of the Audi 80.

Quattro

Audi has considered putting the 2010 concept model of the Quattro into production, but that has yet to happen.

The Audi Quattro was produced from 1980 until 1991. It marked an important accomplishment for Audi. It was the first large-scale production car to have all-wheel drive. All-wheel drive was not a new idea, but no other car manufacturer had been able to produce large numbers of all-wheel-drive cars. All-wheel drive means that all wheels receive **torque** from the engine at the same time. It is common in off-road vehicles. It gives drivers more control and helps them get over more difficult terrain.

1980 Quattro

Engine size	2.1 liters
Number of cylinders	5
Transmission	Manual
Gearbox	5 speeds
0–60 mph (0–97 km/h)	6.3 seconds
Top speed	135 mph (217 km/h)

The Quattro was a two-door coupe with five seats. It had a five-cylinder engine and a top speed of 135 miles per hour (217 km/h). In 2010, for what would be the thirtieth anniversary of the Quattro, Audi showed a new Quattro concept car at the Paris Motor Show. A concept car is a sample car made to show off new technology, features, or model designs. This concept car was an updated version of the original Quattro.

This Audi Quattro won the Rally Monte Carlo in 1984.

TT

The Audi TT began production in 1998 and is still in production. There have been two generations of the TT. The first generation was produced from 1998 until 2006. The second generation started in 2006. There are five different TT models. They are the TT Coupe, the TT Roadster, the TTS Coupe, the TTS Roadster, and the TT RS. The TTS models were introduced in 2008 and are more powerful than the TT versions.

This is a TTS Coupe from the first model year that the more powerful TTS versions of the TT were available.

2013 TT RS

Engine size	2.5 liters
Number of cylinders	5
Transmission	Manual
Gearbox	6 speeds
0–60 mph (0–97 km/h)	4.1 seconds
Top speed	174 mph (280 km/h)

Here is a 2013 TT RS. The "RS" in the name stands for "Rennsport," which is German for "motorsport."

The TT Roadster has a top speed of 130 miles per hour (209 km/h) while the TTS Roadster has a top speed of 155 miles per hour (249 km/h).

The TT RS is the most powerful TT. It has a top speed of 174 miles per hour (280 km/h) and can go from 0 to 60 miles per hour (0–97 km/h) in 4.1 seconds. The TT RS is similar in style to the Audi Quattro. It is very sporty and has all-wheel drive.

A5

There are five different A5 models. They are the A5 Coupe, the S5 Coupe, A5 Cabriolet, S5 Cabriolet, and the RS 5 Coupe. They vary in price and power. The cabriolets are convertibles. The S5 Cabriolet is more powerful than the A5 Convertible. The S5 Cabriolet has a top speed of 155 miles per hour (249 km/h) while the A5 Cabriolet tops out at 130 miles per hour (209 km/h). The A5 series began production in 2005 and is still in production today.

The RS 5 coupe came out in 2010 but was not available in the United States until 2012. The RS 5 is the highest-performing A5. It has a V8 engine and a top speed of 174 miles per hour (280 km/h). The RS 5 has all-wheel drive. Because it is more powerful than the other A5s, the RS 5 has an upgraded suspension and brakes.

RS 5

Engine size	2.5 liters
Number of cylinders	5
Transmission	Manual
Gearbox	6 speeds
0–60 mph (0–97 km/h)	4.1 seconds
Top speed	174 mph (280 km/h)

This is a 2012 Audi A5 Cabriolet.

R8

This is the R8 Spyder. "Spyder" or "Spider" is a name many car companies use for their convertible models.

2012 R8 GT Spyder

Engine size	5.2 liters
Number of cylinders	10
Transmission	Manual
Gearbox	6 speeds
0–60 mph (0–97 km/h)	3.8 seconds
Top speed	198 mph (319 km/h)

The Audi R8 is based on the Lamborghini Gallardo. Lamborghini is an Italian luxury sports car company known for its eye-catching, futuristic designs. The R8 is a supercar. Supercars are fast, powerful, and expensive.

The R8 comes with either a V8 or a V10 engine. The V10 engine is the same as the engine in the Gallardo. The starting price of an R8 is $114,200.

The R8 was first introduced in 2006. Currently, there are four R8 models. They are the R8, the R8 Spyder, the R8 GT, and the R8 GT Spyder. The R8 GT Spyder is the most expensive. It starts at $210,000. It has a V10 engine and a top speed of 198 miles per hour (319 km/h). The R8 GT Spyder is a convertible that is sleek and low to the ground.

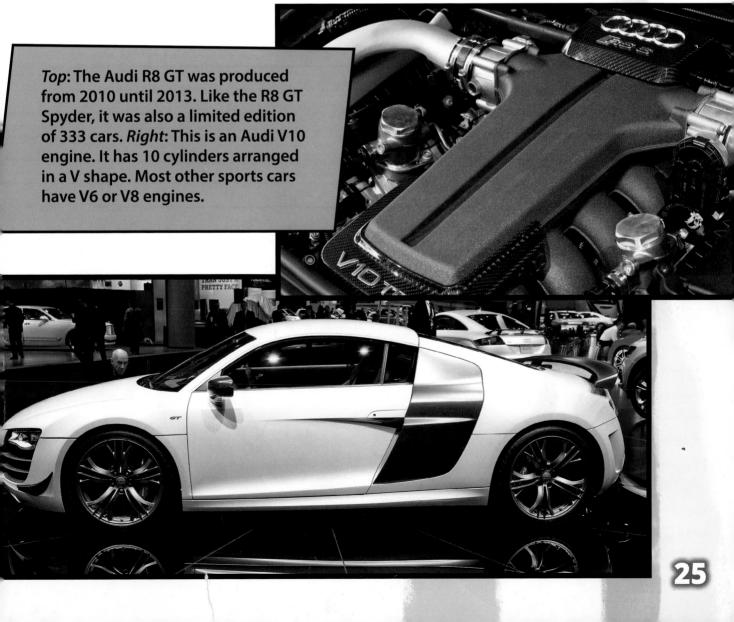

Top: The Audi R8 GT was produced from 2010 until 2013. Like the R8 GT Spyder, it was also a limited edition of 333 cars. *Right*: This is an Audi V10 engine. It has 10 cylinders arranged in a V shape. Most other sports cars have V6 or V8 engines.

Q7

The Q7 is an SUV, or sport-utility vehicle, that was introduced in 2007. These kinds of vehicles are higher off the ground and larger than sports cars. The Q7 has seating for seven passengers. The Q7 has three different engine options with different amounts of torque and horsepower. It is also available with Premium, Premium Plus, or Prestige finishes. The finishes have different technologies, interiors, and wheels. Some of the finishes are parking sensors, keyless entry and ignition, rear-view cameras, and leather upholstery.

The Audi Q7 Prestige has keyless entry. This means the car can be locked and unlocked using a remote control on the car's ignition key.

2013 Q7

Engine size	3 liters
Number of cylinders	6
Transmission	Automatic
Gearbox	8 speeds
0–60 mph (0–97 km/h)	8.5 seconds
Top speed	130 mph (209 km/h)

The Q7 has a V6 engine and all-wheel drive. It has a top speed of 130 miles per hour (209 km/h). The rear seats of the Q7 can fold down, giving drivers lots of cargo space. The Q7 has the style and power of an Audi sports car, but it is roomier and has a more rugged look.

Audi offers its customers a huge number of options. You can choose what style of car you want. You can choose the type of engine you want. You can choose between a convertible or hard top, too. These options make company's cars appeal to a wide variety of people, and suit many different needs. Customers know that no matter what they choose, they will get an expertly engineered car that is stylish and built to last. Starting in

This Audi A3 has the TDI clean diesel engine.

This 2013 Audi S6 is being shown at the North American International Auto Show in Detroit, Michigan.

the spring of 2013, Audi will be offering four new TDI clean diesel models in the United States. Clean diesel engines make fewer **pollutants** than regular diesel engines. They are better for people and the environment.

Audi's wins at endurance racing show that its cars are not only well designed, but also tough and powerful. This attention to style and construction has made Audi a long-lasting brand that will undoubtedly continue to make great cars for a long time.

Comparing Audis

CAR	YEARS MADE	TRANSMISSION	TOP SPEED	FACT
Audi 80	1966–1996	4–speed manual	94 mph (151 km/h)	Around 1,090,690 Audi 80s were built.
Quattro	1980–1991	5–speed manual	135 mph (217 km/h)	"Quattro" means "four" in Italian.
TT	1998–	6–speed manual	174 mph (280 km/h)	The TT is named after a race in Great Britain that NSU used to participate in called the Isle of Man TT.
A5	2005–	6–speed manual	174 mph (280 km/h)	The A5 has rain-sensing windshield wipers. They come on automatically and adjust for how hard it is raining.
R8	2006–	6–speed manual	198 mph (319 km/h)	The R8 GT Spyder and the R8 GT are limited editions.
Q7	2007–	6–speed automatic	130 mph (209 km/h)	The Q7 is the first SUV made by Audi.

Glossary

accelerate (ik-SEH-luh-rayt) To increase in speed.

aerodynamics (er-oh-dy-NA-miks) The study of ways to make things move through the air easily.

coupes (KOOPS) Cars with two doors and hard roofs.

endurance (en-DUR-ints) Strength and the ability to go long distances without getting tired easily.

engineering (en-juh-NEER-ing) Making and using technology.

horsepower (HORS-pow-er) The way an engine's power is measured. One horsepower is the power to lift 550 pounds (250 kg) 1 foot (.3 m) in 1 second.

hybrids (HY-brudz) Cars that have engines that run on gasoline and motors that run on electricity.

innovator (ih-nuh-VAY-ter) A person or group that develops new goods or ideas.

pollutants (puh-LOO-tants) Man-made waste that harms Earth's air, land, or water.

production (pruh-DUK-shun) Made to sell.

sedans (sih-DANZ) Cars that seat four or more people.

technology (tek-NAH-luh-jee) Advanced tools that help people do and make things.

torque (TORK) The force from a car's engine that produces rotation in the drive shaft.

Index

Websites

Due to the changing nature of Internet links, PowerKids Press has developed an online list of websites related to the subject of this book. This site is updated regularly. Please use this link to access the list: www.powerkidslinks.com/smach/audi/